Poetic Ponderings- Streams of Consciousness from a Neurodiverse Nutcase

Luke Mayo

Poetic Ponderings- Streams of
Consciousness from a Neurodiverse Nutcase
© 2023 Luke Mayo

All rights reserved.

Luke Mayo asserts the moral right to be
identified as author of this work.

Presentation by *BookLeaf Publishing*

Web: www.bookleafpub.com

E-mail: info@bookleafpub.com

ISBN: 9789358737820

First edition 2023

This book is dedicated to everyone and anyone who reads it. I hope you find the courage and wisdom to be yourself, unique and creative.

ACKNOWLEDGEMENT

There is a vast array of people who have contributed to my life, and therefore this book. I attempt to acknowledge as many of those people here, in the broadest and sincerest possible terms.

The University of Suffolk, whose English Department has seen fit to bestow upon me a BA (Hons) in English and an MA in Creative and Critical Writing. Both of these academic courses, and the staff and students involved therein, have enabled me to pursue my lifelong passions for creativity. For this, I'm truly grateful.

There have been (almost literally) countless charitable organisations with whom I've worked and volunteered throughout my life. Open Road Visions, the drug recovery service, is one of the most significant. This team of people, and the many others I've met (you know who you are), deserve my heartiest thanks.

My most important expression of gratitude goes to my family, both immediate and extended. They are a wonderfully diverse, flawed, brilliant rabble of people who have supported me, put up with me, guided me, endured me and loved me for the whole of my life. It sounds like a cliché for me to say that I couldn't do this without them, but this particular cliché has a lot of truth in it.

Thank you, thank you, thank you.

PREFACE

Life is all about the pursuit of learning, discovery and love.

We learn about the world and everything in, discovering new, exciting things. This includes ourselves- we are mysterious, complicated, fascinating creatures who are capable of doing great things.

Some of the things we learn can be scary, dangerous, dark, upsetting or all of the above. This doesn't need to stop us from making the best of what we know, and continuing to explore our surroundings.

The poetry in this book is based on some of the things I've discovered in my life, one which centres on my own autistic nature and tendencies. The poetry you'll find written in this book comprises of various neurodiverse observations about this wacky life of ours.

None of my observations are ground-breaking, most of them are probably quite run-of-the-mill, but some of them might be relatable for some of the people who read it. That in itself makes it worth the effort of writing this book.

So please read this book and enjoy it, and feel free to share this with your friends so they might read and enjoy it too. Sharing whatever happiness we find is always a lovely thing to do.

A Different Neural Path

"Why are you like that?"
"What's up with you?"
"I don't get you"
"Why can't you be normal?"
"You can't play with us"

So many questions and comments
I wish I had a good response
But I don't

My lack of response becomes confusion
Confusion becomes misery
Misery becomes apathy
Apathy becomes emptiness
Emptiness becomes darkness

I see a doctor
More questions

"What do you do?"
"Why do you do it?"
"For how long do you do it?"

And so it goes on

After a long wait

The doctor gives me a paper
The paper has words on it
Apparently I'm the words

This explains me
Why I'm like this
What kind of person I am
And it might not be like everyone else

Most people walk a particular neural path
The path I walk is a little bit different

I'm still not sure who I am
That's ok

I'm working it out

A What-If World of Failure

The world is always screaming at me
A constant stream of endless demands

"Find a job and work your socks off"
"Find a partner and have babies"
"Find a home and pay megabucks for it"

I've tried so hard
Every effort has been made
I've laid bare my soul
Offered myself as a sacrifice
Laid down on the altar of society's expectations

There's one thing the world never told me
What if that offering is rejected?

Employers
Love interests
Landlords
What if they turn me down?

What if I'm not what they want?

Like a defective product
Like a boring toy

They toss me aside
No further use for me

But I'm still here
I don't stop existing
My life goes on

What am I supposed to do?
Do I not deserve an explanation?
Is there anything I can do better?
Why am I so worthless to you?
Why has the screaming become silence?

Such is the way society works
It forces its demands when it wants you
It ignores you like you don't exist when it
doesn't
One or the other and no in between

Sadly true and truly sad

Alarmed by the Alarm

Peaceful stillness
Lovely quietness
Simple restfulness
This is sleep

Worlds of freedom
Places with no rules
Reflections of reality
These are dreams

An aggressive intruder
A relentless noise
A source of annoyance

What's this?
It's the alarm clock

Disturber of sleep
Interrupter of dreams
Reminder of daily responsibilities

Such a drastic change
Resting place to action
So abrupt
So rude

Why can't I stay?
Why must life go on?

Worldly duties awaiting me
It all begins with the alarm

Killed by Life Givers

The sun
Light and warmth
We cherish its positivity
Long summer days
Vibrance of nature

The sun sustains our life

Just don't spend too long out there
Those rays can get powerful
Prolonged exposure is deadly
Tanned skinned cells become cancerous

What enables life can end it
When time in the sun becomes too much

The water
Sustaining all forms of life
Flora and fauna require water's nourishment
Humans do as well
Reliant on water's pure salvation

The water keeps us going

Just don't get sucked in
Submerged beneath the darkest depths

Crushed beneath a watery weight
Frozen or boiled by temperature extremes

What supports life can terminate it
When the water we live on suffocates our lungs

Food
A stream of nutrients
The body needs them to work wonders
A healthy intake for functioning organs
Living life to the full

Food guides us through life's journey

Just don't eat too much
Consume too many harmful things
Ingest not enough healthy things
Too much or too little
Food transitions from nourishment to poison

What enables life can snuff it out
When misuse of food's life gifts wrecks the
body

The things we need to live
They can give us a great life
Or they can take life away

It's all about how we use them

Small-Gestured Miracles

"Nobody likes you"
"You ruin everything"
"Things will never get better"

Inner critic comments
We are all familiar with this

We go about our day
Home
Job
Shopping
Friends
Sleep

Those comments
They never leave us alone
Forever haunting our souls

A pit of misery
A future of despair
This is where we reside
No escape

A smile
A friendly nod

"Good morning"
"Nice to see you"

Suddenly
Everything changes
A burst of light emerges

Was someone nice to me?

The day gets better
Our souls feel happier
Life is a bit less hopeless
All because of one small gesture

We all need miracles like these
We can all perform these miracles for each other

Seeking the Right Sensations

In the shower
A deluge of water on skin
A flurry of hot and cold

So much going on
So much internal chaos

Moments later
Things calm down
No more fevered pitch
The shower becomes pleasant

Finding the right clothes
A range of different fabrics
So many to choose from

Some feel intrusive
Like an entrapment on my body
An assault of rough materials

Others are friendly
Like they're giving me a hug

It's just a case of finding the right combination

The food of the day
Needed for survival
An explosion of variety

Flavours
Textures
Aromas

Too hot?
Too spicy?
Too beige?
Too crunchy?
Too runny?

Just right?

A culinary minefield

Seeking the right sensations
It takes time
Finding the right ones is worth it

Walking Wonders

"How do you relax?"

A regular and fair question
To which my answer is easy

I go for a walk

Regular routes
Common destinations
I love the routine
It's a source of comfort

A break from life's anxieties
Just for a moment
It makes all the difference.

I pass people
I see lovely sights
They get my brain thinking
What's the story behind them all?
A rabbit hole of curiosity

New adventures
Different places to explore
Interesting perspectives on life

Walking gives me a chance to do that

If you're looking for me
You'll find me on a walk

Culture of Work

Work, sleep, repeat
An ongoing routine for us all

For something so common
It's also very complicated

Finding a job we're equipped for
Applying for that job in the hopes of getting it
Doing that job daily, weekly, yearly
Endless rounds of complete chaos

And those are the easy bits

Beneath the surface
An array of fires burning

Does the boss hate me?
Will I be fired any minute?
Do my colleagues hate me?
What do they say behind my back?
Will the customers be happy?
Are they on the verge of a tantrum?

And that's just while we're physically at our
jobs

It's even worse when we're not there

Am I being paid enough?
Do I have enough time for other things?
Is my health ok?
Am I wasting my life?

So many questions
So many worries
It's easy to forget
There are good things too

A sense of routine
A regular wage
A chance to do something good

Want to excel in your job?
Turn up and do it
Then you're on to a winner

Missed Communication

I love peace and quiet
I tend not to say very much
I carry about my business
All normal

"What's up with you?"
"Have I upset you?"
"Tell me what's wrong"

What do you mean?
Why is my quietness a problem?

Such is the confusion of communication
Silence is construed as a bad thing
Even if it makes me happy

I talk to people
I try to get my point across
I want them to understand me
So much is riding on it

"Why'd you use that word?"
"That's offensive"
"You're such an idiot"

What was it I said?
I'm sorry you took it that way
I didn't mean any harm
I feel terrible for hurting you

I hope you can forgive me
But you'll probably forget me
While I live with the shame

This is communication
Whatever I say
Whatever I don't say
People treat me like scum
Like a freak

I try to be kind
Be a friend
Be a decent human being
But people use it against me

Alone is not lonely
Lonely is talking with nobody to hear
Sharing yourself with no audience

Those who notice ignore you
Throw your words back at you
Use them to punish you
Twist them to manipulate you

Like a master of puppets

This is missed communication

Unreality TV

We live normal lives
Day after day

We go to work
We go home
We meet friends
We engage in physical love

What else do we do?
We watch the exact same things on TV

Peoples' lives
Peoples' loves
Peoples' privacy
Peoples' souls

They lay it bare for us all
On display for the world to see
Captured and screened through cameras
Packaged and broadcast to a worldwide
audience

In the older sibling house
Insistent on being seen doing not much at all
On the amorous beach

Showing us all their private intimacy

Why do they do it?
Does it make them happy?
Do they get what they're looking for?

Behind the scenes
Misery
Despair
Cruelty
Death

Is it really worth this?

All under the banner of reality TV
But it's not real
Reality is warped
Manipulated
Portrayed to suit a narrative

A narrative which is deadlier than it seems

Welcome to unreality TV

The Bafflement of Insults

Trolls of the internet
Louts of the real world
They all say the same thing

"You're so gay"
"You're such a queer"
And so on
And so on

Is this supposed to be an insult?
Is this the worst they could come up with?
Is being gay really the worst thing?

Members of the gay community
They're some of the best people I've known
Good friends
Kindness and love
It's a privilege to know them

"Gay" is no bad thing

"You're such a girl"
"Man up"
"Such a woman"

And the problem is what?

Women
Some of the strongest members of society
Sources of support and nurturing
They get things done
Unsung heroes

Womanhood is a good thing

Want to throw around insults?
Look in the mirror
Vileness
Bigotry
Hatred
Jealousy
Lies

The worst insults of them all
And the trolls can't see them in themselves

Routine Rebellion

I'm a lover of routine
Planning out my days
Same tasks
Same time
Repeat again and again

I like to know what's coming

A flurry of planners
Diaries
Calendars
To-do lists

I like the achievement
Getting through each item
Until the agenda is complete

But sometimes
Deviation becomes part of the plan

Adding new things
Finding new priorities
Shedding old responsibilities

This is how life works

Change is inevitable
Embracing it is a power move
This is what I try to do

When you have a plan
It's easier to rebel against it

This is ok
As long as you still achieve good things

Picking Out A Lifestyle

Every human has a common denominator
We all have a life to live
A path to follow

The path we choose
It's as varied as the number of humans

Another commonality
Whichever path you choose
Hate will come at you by other paths

Health
Diet
Exercise
Body type
Mental health

So many facts
So many opinions
So many categories
So many options

One thing we know
Self-care is important

How you do it is up to you
Until someone disagrees
That's when the slanging starts
Insults are flung
Savagery is displayed

All for picking a lifestyle for yourself

Money
How much?
How little?
How do you get it?

Some are ambitious for it
Some have far too much
Some have nowhere near enough
Some are content

Whichever box you fit in
Someone in the other boxes will hate you

You're a lazy bum
You're a greedy grubber
You aren't trying hard enough
You're obsessed with wealth

Here's a question
Why can't we mind our own business?

The more we slander the other paths
The less progress we make on our own

Lifestyles
Live your own
Leave the others alone
A happy life will be yours

Perchance Not to Dream

Sleep
Rest for a weary body
A chance for the brain to pause

Except the brain doesn't pause
It keeps going

An endless sequence of images
Loosely tethered to reality
Deepest, darkest emotions
Brought to the fore
Paraded like a freak show

I only wanted to escape the tiredness
I'll be more tired when I wake up

Can you imagine if we didn't dream?
A brain completely still
No whimsical movements
No flights of fancy
No personal revelations

Empty silence

Dreams can be weird
No dreams would be weirder

The Age of Documentation

Endless photos
Birthdays
Holidays
Families
Meals

Social media
Opinions
News
Experiences

Tattoos
Names
Icons
Dates

Important things
Not to be lost to time
History notes these things we do
Everything gets documented
This is the age we live in

Good things
Bad things
Joys

Misery
Horror

When we grow old
When our memory deteriorates
These memorials will remain
They keep us company in our elderly years

For this is the age of documentation

The Worship of Shock

Everywhere I look
Every industry of public display
Extreme performances before my eyes

Musical entertainment
Explicit lyrics
Brazen nudity
Pornographic lewdness
Horrific stunts
Masquerading as showmanship

Comedy
Jokes so dark you need a torch
Traumas and brutality picked apart
Holocausts
Abortion
Sex offences
Fair game if it's funny

Media figures
Spreading hate for honesty's sake
Everything in the world is evil
Nobody is safe from the glare of judgement
All eyes are spying for mistakes

Humanity thrives on this
Every person on the planet
They either gorge on it
Or they revile it
Nobody ignores it
For this is impossible

The greater the shock
The greater the glory

Welcome to today's worship

Political Prattery

Extreme reactions
Rage
Despair
Panic
Elicited by a single word

Politics

The people in government
Their legacy is bunglement
Floundering failures
Health disasters
Educational woes
Financial catastrophes

Deaths multiplying
Populations languishing in misery
Prisons of buildings and minds
Criminals on the streets
Good folks entrapped
All because of those at the top

Us folks watching
We love to joke
We love to moan

We love to poke
We love to moan

"Have you got any better ideas?"
"Maybe you should take charge"

Horror ensues

As bad as things are
Nobody wants to take the mantle
For that would be worse
Being responsible for a nation's problems
All for fame and fortune

Political prattery
Better to watch it than do it

Metaphors and Meanings

You shine like the brightest star

Is that so?
But stars are lonely
They obliterate anything too close
They die away eventually
This isn't what I want

But I can still be great
I can still do wonderful things
I can still be a good person
I can still make life warmer
I can still shine a light in the world
I can still inspire people

You're as pretty as a flower

Am I?
Flowers are so different
Some are dangerous
Some are poisonous
All wilt and die
Not sure if this is me

But I am still beautiful

I am still a bringer of joy
I am still a sign of the world's good things
I am still a lovely work of nature

Metaphors
Not to be taken literally
But to be enjoyed and appreciated

We people are to be appreciated too

Demonstrations of Love

Every person is the same
In that we feel love for each other
Every person is unique
In how we express our love

Some of us can simply say it
We know the right words
We know how to say them
We know the right time
The right way
The right tone

People like me
The words don't work so well
So we find other methods

"Look at this thing I made you"
"This thing you love- I'll take you there"
"I'll sit with you quietly"
"I'll let you speak while I listen"
"Here's your space to simply exist with validity"

For the right person
This is the world
A transition from darkness to light

No need for "I love you"
Those words say it without saying it

If I can't find the right words to demonstrate my
love
Let me find the right actions instead

Mental Shutdown

Too many people
Too many demands
Too many insults
Just one brain

Problems rise
So do emotions
Stress
Frustration
Hopelessness

I don't know where the limit is
I just know I've passed it

The emotions become so much
They feel like nothing
The brain is so full
It feels empty
The problems become so large
I can't see them any more

My battered brain
Stimulated again and again
Active to the point of catatonia
You have reached your destination

Welcome to mental shutdown

Motivational Madness

So many nice words
"Love"
"Dreams"
"Hard work"
"Satisfied"
"Friend"

They're nice to hear
Put them in any order
Everyone wants to be told them

Put them with a nice picture
A mountain
A field
A beach
A flower

Dialogue and images
The right combination makes a perfect aesthetic

Add a sound
Soothing music
A cool breeze
Birdsong
River babbles

Post these three things together
Any social media outlet
A thousand likes will come your way

Were you trying to motivate me?
Do you want me to accomplish things?
Whoops, too late

Too bad the visual and audio wonders didn't
help

We all have the power to do good things
We don't need a picture party to instruct us
We just do the stuff
We'll get to it at the right time
Give us a minute

Don't overload me with fake positivity
Just let me do what I need to do